SAN FRANCI

THE CITY AT A GLANCE

CW00687235

Transamerica Pyramid
At 260m tall, the city's most recog
tower is no longer home to the Tra
Corporation, but the moniker has stuck.
See p013

City Hall
A Beaux Arts gem with a gilded dome, City Hall
needed a decade of restoration after the 1989
earthquake to return it to its former glory.
1 Dr Carlton B Goodlett Place

United States Mint
Built on a hilltop in 1937, and evoking a prison,
Gilbert Stanley Underwood's forbidding block
of stripped classicism has proved an effective
deterrent to any potential bank robbers.
155 Hermann Street

Market Street
Running diagonally from The Castro up to the
waterfront Ferry Building, this is a main route
for San Francisco's famous fleet of cable cars.

Salesforce Tower
Despite severe quake risk, Pelli Clarke Pelli's
326m skyscraper is symbolic of the upwards
direction planners have had to take to squeeze
10,000 new residents a year into 121 sq km.
See p072

SFMOMA
Snøhetta's eagerly anticipated SFMOMA
revamp and extension was unveiled in 2016.
It is grabbing all the headlines, and rightly so.
See p026

Bay Bridge
This 7,180m-long crossing to Oakland is two
spans in one, connected by Yerba Buena
Island. The rebuilding of its eastern section,
which was completed in 2013, cost $6.4bn.

INTRODUCTION
THE CHANGING FACE OF THE URBAN SCENE

From Gold Rush miners to hippies and now internet visionaries, dreamers have long flocked to San Francisco. Endowed with a can-do mindset and a knockout setting, it is one of the most alluring and cosmopolitan cities in America. Less daunting and aggressive than New York, and more manageable than Los Angeles, its well-defined districts, from monied Nob Hill to hip The Mission, are easy to navigate. Its numerous anomalies – Victorian architecture and radical new-builds cheek by jowl; the 19th-century cable cars running alongside self-driving vehicles; social media billionaires mixing with social activists – make for an enthralling experience.

The tech boomtown is forever looking for the next IPO, despite concern about the effects of this wealth. Rocketing house prices, the displacement of the working class and rising homelessness cause spirited debate. Since the controversial Twitter tax break of 2011, Mid-Market is now *the* place to live for those who can afford it, and best encapsulates this paradox – soaring above shuttered storefronts are glossy condo complexes that are out of reach for most locals.

San Francisco's dynamic cultural life is cause for optimism, from the grassroots revival of Dogpatch and The Tenderloin to the rebirth of SFMOMA (see p026). Infrastructure and public spaces are also being upgraded; the Transbay Transit Center (see p072) came into operation in 2017. Add to this the city's status as the world leader in biotech and digital innovation, and there's hope for a bright future.

ESSENTIAL INFO
FACTS, FIGURES AND USEFUL ADDRESSES

TOURIST OFFICE
900 Market Street
T 391 2000
www.sftravel.com

TRANSPORT
Airport transfer to city centre
Trains depart regularly from 5am until
midnight on weekdays, and from 6.30am
on Saturdays and 8am on Sundays. The
journey takes approximately 30 minutes
www.bart.gov
Cable cars and trolleybuses
Muni
www.sfmta.com
Car hire
Avis
T 929 2555
Taxi
Yellow Cab Cooperative
T 333 3333
Tourist card
A nine-day CityPASS ($89) includes travel
on Muni and free entry to select attractions
such as the de Young Museum (see p031)
www.citypass.com/san-francisco

EMERGENCY SERVICES
Emergencies
T 911
24-hour pharmacy
Walgreens
459 Powell Street
T 984 0793
www.walgreens.com

CONSULATES
British Consulate
Suite 850
1 Sansome Street
T 617 1300
www.gov.uk/government/world/usa

POSTAL SERVICES
Post office
150 Sutter Street
T 626 2932
Shipping
UPS
T 800 742 5877

BOOKS
**Cool Gray City of Love: 49 Views of San
Francisco** by Gary Kamiya (Bloomsbury)
Frank Lloyd Wright and San Francisco
by Paul V Turner (Yale University)
Tales of the City
by Armistead Maupin (Black Swan)
This is San Francisco
by Miroslav Sasek (Universe)

WEBSITES
Art/Design
www.sfarts.org
www.sfmoma.org
Newspaper
www.sfgate.com

EVENTS
FOG Design+Art
www.fogfair.com
San Francisco Design Week
www.sfdesignweek.org

COST OF LIVING
Taxi from SFO Airport to Union Square
$55
Cappuccino
$4
Packet of cigarettes
$8
Daily newspaper
$1.50
Bottle of champagne
$65

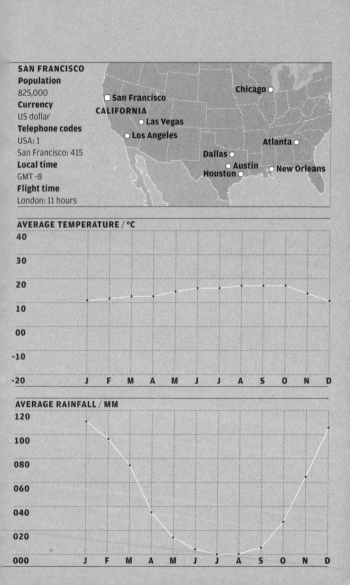

SAN FRANCISCO
Population
825,000
Currency
US dollar
Telephone codes
USA: 1
San Francisco: 415
Local time
GMT -8
Flight time
London: 11 hours

San Francisco
CALIFORNIA
Chicago
Las Vegas
Los Angeles
Atlanta
Dallas
Austin
Houston
New Orleans

AVERAGE TEMPERATURE / °C

40												
30												
20												
10												
00												
-10												
-20	J	F	M	A	M	J	J	A	S	O	N	D

AVERAGE RAINFALL / MM

120												
100												
080												
060												
040												
020												
000	J	F	M	A	M	J	J	A	S	O	N	D

NEIGHBOURHOODS
THE AREAS YOU NEED TO KNOW AND WHY

To help you navigate the city, we've chosen the most interesting districts (see below and the map inside the back cover) and colour-coded our featured venues, according to their location; those venues that are outside these areas are not coloured.

NORTH BEACH/CHINATOWN
In the city's north-eastern corner, where the hilltop art deco Coit Tower (see p012) keeps a beady eye on proceedings, North Beach is packed with restaurants, theatres and comedy venues. Chinese businesses cluster along Stockton and Grant Avenues.

NOB HILL
This is where the gold and silver barons flocked in the 1800s, in order to be above the hoi polloi. The neighbourhood now overlooks Russian Hill and the Financial District. Grace Cathedral (1100 California Street, T 749 6300) is a notable resident. Refuel at Lord Stanley (see p048).

DOGPATCH
A former industrial wasteland colonised by creatives, Dogpatch is the latest buzz district, headlined by art hub Minnesota Street Project (see p068). Also check out the Museum of Craft and Design (2569 3rd Street, T 773 0303). Dining options include elevated Hawaiian restaurant 'Āina (900 22nd Street, T 814 3815).

SOMA
South of Market Street, or SoMa, is the city's cultural epicentre, encompassing SFMOMA (see p026) and the Museum of the African Diaspora (685 Mission Street, T 358 7200), inventive architecture like the Federal Building (see p014) and the Jewish Museum (see p027), and upmarket hotels, notably the funky Zetta (see p016).

FINANCIAL DISTRICT
Big business has attracted some of the poshest bars and digs in town, exemplified by The Battery (see p021), and refined restaurants such as Quince (see p040). One of the skyscrapers casting shadows is the Transamerica Pyramid (see p013).

THE TENDERLOIN/UNION SQUARE
Few other areas capture San Francisco's dichotomy better than this juxtaposition of Union Square, with its aspirational department stores and Foster + Partners' Apple flagship (300 Post Street, T 486 4800), and the rough-around-the-edges urban underbelly of The Tenderloin.

THE MISSION
Some of the city's hippest restaurants, from Lazy Bear (see p046) to AL's Place (see p050), and creative retailers (see p083), have moved in among the vibrant Latino community and lively street art. The area is named after Mission Dolores (3321 16th Street, T 621 8203), the oldest building in San Francisco, dating from 1791.

HAYES VALLEY
Located between Alamo Square and the Civic Center, this fashionable zone radiates from Hayes Street. Its multitude of venues includes fashion boutique Acrimony (see p095), florist-cum-magazine store Birch (564 Hayes Street, T 626 6860), eaterie Little Gem (see p024) and drinking hole Smuggler's Cove (see p040).

LANDMARKS

THE SHAPE OF THE CITY SKYLINE

San Francisco is something of a landmark itself, embedded in the American psyche, and imbued with effortless cool and charm. It's also a sight to behold, especially when viewed from the Bay or the immense Golden Gate Bridge (overleaf). Surrounded by water and pushed this way and that by its many hills, the city's rollercoaster streets and skyline never fail to evoke drama, its high-rises poking through the morning fog or glinting in the Californian sun.

Hemmed in on three sides by the coast, San Francisco has always grown vertically, the only way it could. As a result, the splendour of the 19th-century architecture that survived the calamitous 1906 earthquake (much of the city was completely destroyed by the time the resulting fire was put out) has been overshadowed downtown by a slew of bland, formulaic skyscrapers. One that does stand out from the crowd, however, is the gleaming Transamerica Pyramid (see p013), designed by William L Pereira – it can be seen from most neighbourhoods, acting as a useful orientation point.

The city has its fair share of unusual landmarks too. For instance, Lombard Street draws coachloads of tourists with its sine-wave hairpins. And although the Dutch Windmill (1691 John F Kennedy Drive) at Ocean Beach is not as well known internationally, it is beloved by locals, who cherish it as a reminder of a time when this place was just a demure backwater half-covered in sand dunes. *For full addresses, see Resources.*

Golden Gate Bridge

One of the planet's great architectural icons, the Golden Gate Bridge is instantly recognisable and, when seen first-hand, its power remains undiminished. The 2.7km structure spans the strait linking San Francisco Bay to the Pacific, joining the city with Marin County, its two towers rising 227m above the water. Finished in 1937, four years after the foundations were anchored, it was originally going to be painted black and yellow, but leading architect Irving F Morrow insisted on the now-irreplaceable international orange. The bridge seems to accentuate its own myth, as it's often shrouded in fog rolling in off the ocean, or bathed in dappled Californian sunshine. Driving across it in a convertible is surely one of the best experiences in the world.

T 426 5220, www.goldengatebridge.org

Coit Tower

The 64m art deco Coit Tower stands proud on top of Telegraph Hill's Pioneer Park, and affords visitors some of the finest vistas of the Bay from its open-air viewing arcade. It was built using funds left to the city in 1929 by a wealthy financier's widow, Lillie Hitchcock Coit, an eccentric who smoked cigars, and dressed as a man to gamble in the restricted North Beach dens. The three nested concrete cylinders were designed by architects Arthur Brown Jr and Henry Howard and unveiled in 1933. Local lore has it that the shape resembles the nozzle of a hose, as Coit was an avid supporter of San Francisco's busy fire service (all those wooden buildings). Inside, a succession of murals by local artists, some paying tribute to Diego Rivera, provides a socio-economic commentary on the Great Depression.
1 Telegraph Hill Boulevard, T 249 0095

Transamerica Pyramid

William L Pereira's 48-floor skyscraper, which was completed in 1972, dominates the Financial District and beyond, serving as a handy navigational aid. Nicknamed Pereira's Prick by its detractors, it faced fierce opposition during its planning and construction, but the building is now as synonymous with San Francisco as the Golden Gate Bridge. The Transamerica Pyramid is covered in crushed quartz, which gives it a white appearance, and when seen from across the Bay on a sunny day, it does appear to glow. Following the 9/11 attacks, an observation deck towards the 260m summit was closed, but large video screens in the plaza-level visitors' centre display live views from cameras that are mounted at the top of the spire.

600 Montgomery Street,
www.pyramidcenter.com

Federal Building

This slender government edifice was designed by Morphosis, architects of the Caltrans District 7 headquarters in downtown Los Angeles. The most radical architecture to appear in the heart of the city for decades, the 2007 Federal Building divided local opinion, but a year after opening, it won a Design Award from San Francisco's AIA chapter. *Mission Street/7th Street*

HOTELS

WHERE TO STAY AND WHICH ROOMS TO BOOK

The notorious housing shortage has had a regrettable side effect: a staid hotel scene. However, recent openings and renovations have shaken things up with some much-needed design nous.

Almost all of the action is concentrated within a few blocks in any direction of Union Square, summed up by the 2017 relaunch of a 1928 hotel as the minimalist Tilden (345 Taylor Street, T 673 2332), with its buzzy cocktail bar/diner The Douglas Room. The Zeppelin (opposite) had arrived the previous year, and here you'll also find Hotel G (see p022) and the veteran Clift (495 Geary Street, T 775 4700), spruced up by Philippe Starck. In The Tenderloin is the Phoenix (601 Eddy Street, T 776 1380), a Palm Springs-style 1960s motor lodge, long a bastion of retro cool. To the north are swanky The Ritz-Carlton (600 Stockton Street, T 296 7465) and the Mystic (417 Stockton Street, T 400 0500), set in a Victorian building; its Burritt Room has a film-noir vibe. And in SOMA are the hip Zetta (opposite), the eco-friendly InterContinental (888 Howard Street, T 616 6500) and the stately St Regis (125 3rd Street, T 284 4000).

To experience a different area, try The Buchanan (see p018) in Lower Pacific Heights, the Vitale (see p020), by the Bay Bridge, and The Battery (see p021) in the Financial District. Or escape from it all completely at Inn at the Presidio (42 Moraga Avenue, T 800 7356), a converted army quarters in the Golden Gate Recreation Area. *For full addresses and room rates, see Resources.*

Zeppelin

The Viceroy Group opened the Zetta (T 543 8555) in 2013 and it's still a brogrammers' paradise, kitted out with Bluetooth, Jambox speakers, Nintendo, and retro-nostalgic pop art portraits made from floppy disks. The Zeppelin is the 2016 follow-up, also by Dawson Design Associates, comprising 196 rooms carved out of a press club and inn. Exposed brick, wooden floors and ornate cornices contrast with a games room with a quick-shot basketball wall, shuffleboard, and electronic bingo synced to a sound system. The lobby café/bar has an LED-lit cage with 160 bottles of gin, and is daubed with graffiti visible only in black light. Book the Deluxe Suite (above) for its fireplace, custom furniture, record deck, psychedelic bathroom, artworks and hoodie-like robes.
545 Post Street, T 563 0303,
www.viceroyhotelsandresorts.com

The Buchanan

On the Fillmore/Japantown/Pacific Heights borders, The Buchanan tasked designer Nicole Hollis with reinterpreting the area's storied jazz haunts, Asian heritage and beat-era vibe at this 2015 launch. Its clubby lobby (opposite) features a wall of charred whisky barrel staves, work by local artists, including Aleksandra Zee (see p064), hung on midnight-green panelling, Kelly Ording's fan-motif mural behind reception, and 3,000 suspended bottles that play with the light. Bedrooms, such as the King Balcony (above), pick up the themes in quirks like the TVs set in easels, pinstripe drapes and shibori-print pillows, although bathrooms are rather spartan. On-site Mums (T 931 6986) specialises in *shabu shabu*, and it's an easy stroll to The Progress (see p049). *1800 Sutter Street, T 921 4000, www.thebuchananhotel.com*

Hotel Vitale

By the water at the eastern end of Mission Street, the Vitale's loudest calling card is its views of Alcatraz, Treasure Island and the Oakland Bay Bridge, beautifully framed by Leo Villareal's 25,000-LED installation at night. Book a Deluxe Panoramic Circular Suite for the 180-degree vistas from the bed and bath, or a Terrace Suite, which have a private patio with lounge furniture and heat lamps, while the rooftop Spa Vitale (T 278 3788) offers two bamboo-encased hot tubs available to allcomers. Restaurant Americano (T 278 3777) serves Italian cuisine, and its circular Lido Lounge (above) is popular for happy-hour drinks among the local techie crowd. Opposite is the Ferry Building (see p052) and refined Vietnamese The Slanted Door (T 861 8032).
*8 Mission Street, T 278 3700,
www.hotelvitale.com*

The Battery

This discreet 15-key genuine boutique hotel is attached to a members-only social club. The rooms have an old-school, debonair feel thanks to local interior designer Ken Fulk, with hardwood floors, art displayed on the walls and stone-tiled bathrooms. Our favourite, the Lounge Suite (above), showcases the building's brick bones and has a separate living area decked out with vintage furniture, and The Penthouse is all steel, glass and firepits, with a rooftop patio affording a swoon-worthy panorama. However, the biggest draw will most likely be access to the club, with its wine cellar, gym, spa and steam room, bars, including The Musto, a symphony in cerused oak, and restaurant The Living Room, which serves chef Nicolai Lipscomb's Cali-Med cuisine. *717 Battery Street, T 230 8000, www.thebatterysf.com/hotel*

Hotel G

This 1908 building gained an art deco extension in 1939 but its original features were masked by a succession of heavy-handed hotel fit-outs. It wasn't until 2014, due to a restoration by Hun Aw Studio that shed daylight on the cross-bracing, hex-tile flooring and a glorious cast-iron staircase, that Hotel G nailed the formula. A vintage feel continues in the 150 rooms (Greatest King, right), where walnut finishes, woven rugs, oversized tufted headboards, patches of vintage floral wallpaper and salvaged school chairs are filtered through a neutral palette. Waxed canvas and leather multi-pocket hanging pouches from Strawfoot Handmade make a stylish alternative to a minibar. Downstairs speakeasy Benjamin Cooper serves oysters and cocktails, like the Black Rye, mixed with whisky, brandy, bitters and a slice of blow-torched apple.
386 Geary Street, T 738 0589,
www.hotelgsanfrancisco.com

24 HOURS

SEE THE BEST OF THE CITY IN JUST ONE DAY

San Francisco is easy to explore; you can cross the city by car in half an hour. Public transport is efficient, and cable cars and trams provide a fun and historic way to get around town. If the weather's fine, then do take in the views from the water as well as land.

There are myriad ways you could spend your day quite apart from the itinerary listed here. An indie scene is thriving in the old warehouses of The Mission and Potrero Hill, notably in the galleries on Utah Street (see p070), and Dogpatch, where Minnesota Street Project (see p068) hosts the established and the nascent. No doubt SFMOMA (see p026) will be a priority, and you could combine a visit with lunch at In Situ (T 941 6050), where 80 world-renowned chefs have allowed Corey Lee (see p053) to replicate their signature dishes. Alternatively, refuel on your way to the de Young Museum (see p031) at super-healthy and flavourful Little Gem (400 Grove Street, T 914 0501) or organic Mexican canteen Nopalito (1224 9th Avenue, T 233 9966), where the almond horchatas are legendary.

Note that if you are trying to squeeze everything in, tours of The David Ireland House (see p034) last 90 minutes, but the Center for the Book (see p036) closes at 5.30pm, unless you have reserved one of its evening workshops. One of the most sought-after, albeit pricey, dinner engagements is Saison (see p038). Knock the edges off with late cocktails at ABV (3174 16th Street, T 400 4748). *For full addresses, see Resources.*

08.30 Mazarine Coffee

Founder Hamid Rafati was inspired by the egalitarian spirit of Bibliotèque Mazarine in Paris when naming this slick venture. Boor Bridges has accessorised the raw concrete, rough plaster and exposed-pipe shell, part of an office block, with wood, brass and marble, and tiled alcoves that 'mimic the rhythm of library shelving' in deep blue (mazarine) hues. The espresso, nitro cold brew, and drip coffee comes from a rotating list of roasters including local favourite Ritual. Toast might be a breakfast staple but it's one that San Francisco takes very seriously, and here it comes topped with watermelon radish, or fig jam, ricotta and sea salt. Another champion is The Mill (T 345 1953), where treats include dark rye with cream cheese, pesto and pine nuts.
720 Market Street, T 398 7700,
www.mazarinecoffee.com

09.30 SFMOMA

After a three-year hiatus, SFMOMA was rebooted in 2016 with a new 10-storey wing by Snøhetta that tripled the exhibition area yet manages to be unobtrusive. It is most distinctive on its sinewy east facade, which is clad in 700 fibreglass-reinforced polymer panels that emulate the Bay Area's fog and waves. It is a stark departure from Mario Botta's original 1995 postmodern building that comprises a striped cylinder dissecting a red-brick body, yet the two meld well without obvious demarcations inside. Two entrances on different streets enable an easy flow through at ground level, where Richard Serra's massive *Sequence* is visible through glass walls. Six outdoor terraces include a sculpture gallery with the largest living wall in the US. Closed Wednesdays.
151 3rd Street, T 357 4000,
www.sfmoma.org

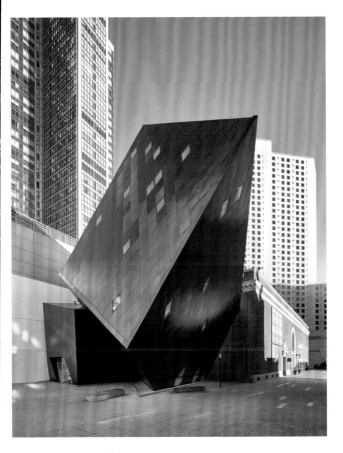

11.00 Contemporary Jewish Museum

Unmistakably the work of Daniel Libeskind, the Jewish Museum evokes a 3D rhombus that's fallen from the sky into a corner of a heritage building. He was inspired by the Hebrew toast *L'Chaim*, meaning 'To Life!', and the concept is borne out on various levels. This was the city's main power plant until 1924 (energy = life), a 1907 neoclassical statement by Willis Polk, and Libeskind's 2008 extension traces the shape of the two letters that form the word *chai*. Clad in luminous dark-blue steel diamonds, *chet* is a slanted rectangle that forms the lobby and *yud* is the 20m-tall signature structure, with 36 irregular windows (multiples of 18 are said to be lucky). Its eclectic exhibitions invariably fail to live up to the ambition of the architecture. Closed Wednesdays.
736 Mission Street, T 655 7800,
www.thecjm.org

11.30 Onsen

Symbolic of The Tenderloin's upturn, Onsen is a car-repair shop turned *sento* (Japanese bathhouse). Sunny Simmons and Caroline Smith have preserved the brick shell of the early 1900s building but transformed the interior, using salvaged redwood and Douglas fir, American clay, factory-second concrete sinks, and details such as antique shower fixtures and sashiko-stitched noren curtains. The soaking tub, carved out of the mechanics' pit, is kept at 40°C and fits eight people, there is also a sauna and a subway-tiled steam room, and massages and acupuncture are offered. Mixed days are Friday to Monday; closed Tuesdays. An intimate bistro, serving healthy, colourful Japan-meets-California dishes, and tea, cocktails and sake, opens for dinner only. *466 Eddy Street, T 441 4987, www.onsensf.com*

12.30 Jessica Silverman Gallery

Inspired by her grandparents, who donated their collection of Fluxus art to New York's MoMA, Jessica Silverman was just 20 when she launched her fledgling venture while studying in LA in 2003. In San Francisco, along with other gallerists, she was drawn first to Dogpatch and then The Tenderloin, and expanded here in 2013 to a 280 sq m corner plot of a storied 1907 hotel (now a housing project). In a space conceived by designer Charles de Lisle, she champions emerging talent of all ages. Her roster features rising stars like Istanbul's Hayal Pozanti, as well as Londoner Isaac Julien ('Vintage', above) and state-based artists such as Christopher Badger, photographer Tammy Rae Carland and painter Dashiell Manley. Closed Sundays and Mondays. *488 Ellis Street, T 255 9508, www.jessicasilvermangallery.com*

14.00 de Young Museum

One of Herzog & de Meuron's most thought-provoking designs, the de Young is covered in perforated and textured copper, which creates the effect of light filtering through trees. As the facade ages and acquires a patina, it blends further into Golden Gate Park. Tiers of windows, and unexpected angles and apertures, blur the boundary between interior and exterior. However, the galleries are unobtrusive, yielding the spotlight to the collection of American paintings, sculpture and decorative arts from the 17th century to the present day, as well as contemporary craft, and pieces from Africa, Oceania and the Americas. On the north-east side, a 44m-high tower has a glass observation deck that affords great views over west San Francisco.
50 Hagiwara Tea Garden Drive,
T 750 3600, www.deyoung.famsf.org

15.15 California Academy of Sciences
As if it weren't enough to have a Herzog & de Meuron project (see p031) in Golden Gate Park, Renzo Piano's striking, almost camouflaged intervention across the plaza, opened in 2008, is one of the country's most environmentally friendly structures, and certainly merits a gander while you are here. The academy combines research with education, and comprises a natural history museum, an aquarium and more.

Piano 'lifted up a piece of the park and put a building underneath', creating a 10m-high, undulating living roof covered in 1.7m indigenous plants in biodegradable coconut-fibre containers. There's a concave glass canopy over the lobby and two main domes above the rainforest exhibition and planetarium that are dotted with skylights. *55 Music Concourse Drive, T 379 8000, www.calacademy.org*

16.00 The David Ireland House

David Ireland bought the rundown 1886 Edwardian house 500 Capp Street on his city homecoming in 1975, and turned the renovation and the property itself into an evolving work of art. It became a focal point of the 1980s Bay Area conceptualist movement. Ireland liked to call himself a 'post-discipline artist', influenced by Zen and postmodernism. His use of everyday objects can be seen in *Broom Collection with Boom* (opposite), while installations like *The View from This Window*, a copper-covered window with an audio of Ireland describing the vista, reveal his humour. You can only visit on a tour, held at 11am, 2pm and 4pm, Wednesdays to Saturdays. Shows by other artists in the converted garage (above) are free on Saturday afternoons. *500 Capp Street, T 872 9240, www.500cappstreet.org*

17.00 San Francisco Center for the Book

This letterpress printing and bookmaking school is a celebration of publishing and typography, and offers workshops on every aspect of the craft (book ahead for classes). The venerable non-profit moved into an old warehouse in 2013, installing all manner of presses, a platemaking lab, a bookbinding studio, an extensive type collection and a gallery (above) that hosts shows such as a retrospective on influential designer Hedi Kyle. The store sells mini concept books created by artists. Dubbed DoReMi (it's between Dogpatch, Potrero Hill and The Mission), this district is on the up. Check out the Wattis Institute for Contemporary Arts (T 355 9670), located in a former bus depot, and the Anchor Brewing Company (T 863 8350), one of the first in the US. *375 Rhode Island Street, T 565 0545, www.sfcb.org*

18.00 Street art

The first artist to decorate the city's walls was Mexican muralist Diego Rivera, whose clever, self-referential 1931 *The Making of a Fresco Showing the Building of a City* is located in the San Francisco Art Institute (800 Chestnut Street). Thanks to a proud history of counterculture, there are now more than 1,000 pieces of street art to see. About half are in The Mission, where Balmy Alley has been a political canvas since the 1970s, and Clarion Alley is a hotbed of anti-gentrification sentiment and a reflection of the zeitgeist. You'll also find plenty in The Tenderloin. Locally based talents to look out for include Apexer, Rigo 23, Zio Ziegler and Victor Reyes, who has wrapped entire buildings (1420 Harrison Street, above) in his intricate graphics, and hidden every letter of the alphabet through The Mission. *www.reyes78.com*

20.30 Saison

Serving ultra-local New American cuisine, Saison won its third Michelin star in 2014. The previous year it had moved into the California Electric Light Company Building, dating from 1888, one of the few survivors of the 1906 earthquake. Architects Michael Gibson and Samaha+Hart, in collaboration with interior designer Jiun Ho, conceived the space, suspending lights from an iron framework and exposing the oak beams. The astronomically priced tasting menu is one of the most expensive in the country but the food is a revelation. Chef Joshua Skenes uses fish, aged meats and foraged vegetables in his creations, often topping them with caviar or abalone. Menus aren't released in advance, but that's part of the experience. Allow more than three hours for a meal and book at least 60 days ahead.
178 Townsend Street, T 828 7990, www.saisonsf.com

URBAN LIFE
CAFÉS, RESTAURANTS, BARS AND NIGHTCLUBS

An oceanside location and the verdant land outside the city grant chefs access to some of the finest raw ingredients in the country, not to mention the state's excellent wine and craft beers, and it's perhaps no surprise that San Francisco has the highest number of restaurants per capita in the US. Sourcing local, seasonal produce is not just a trend but a bare minimum requirement for any place worth its salt. Farmers' markets, like the one on Tuesdays, Thursdays and Saturdays at the Ferry Terminal, supply not only high-end kitchens like Saison (see p038) and Quince (470 Pacific Avenue, T 775 8500), but also mom-and-pop eateries. Moving around the city, Off the Grid (www.offthegrid.com) is a congregation of food trucks, where big names experiment and fledgling cooks cut their teeth, and is a barometer of the gastronomic future.

Appealing bars are plentiful too. Our picks are away from the beaten path but worth the effort: try idiosyncratic hangouts such as quirky Smuggler's Cove (650 Gough Street, T 869 1900), and Trick Dog (3010 20th Street, T 471 2999), which overhauls its drinks concept every six months. The best nightclubs are not immediately obvious either, nor as open as in London or New York, but there are plenty of eclectic and interesting venues to be found. Bergerac (316 11th Street, T 255 9440) is a happening cocktail lounge where you can keep the party going upstairs at Audio (T 481 0556). *For full addresses, see Resources.*

Mister Jiu's

This Chinatown eaterie has been a hotspot since opening in 2016. Chef Brandon Jew offers a five-course, family-style Cantonese tasting menu featuring dishes such as crab cake with banana, coconut and peanut, and tea-smoked duck with crab sauce, carrot custard and pea tendrils. From the bar, try the Wealth cocktail, mixed with scotch, rye, Cardamaro, lapsang tea and apple. Prolific interior architects Boor Bridges kept the brass lotus chandeliers from the previous kitschy incarnation and overhauled the rest of it, instilling a midcentury feel. Three custom tables fitted with Lazy Susans and ringed by Brazilian Aristeu Pires' 'Duda' chairs anchor the room, and ceramics add warmth. A focal point is the huge drawing *La Plaza Blanca* by local artist Afton Love. *28 Waverly Place, T 857 9688, www.misterjius.com*

Sightglass

Brothers Jerad and Justin Morrison set up Sightglass in 2009 as a rickety espresso service cart behind a roll-up garage door. Over the next two years, they transformed the century-old warehouse into a spacious café and roastery, specialising in artisanal coffees sourced from farmers in Rwanda or Nicaragua. Success has led to a second outlet on 20th Street in The Mission (T 641 1043) and a third in SFMOMA (see p026).

The Douglas fir, steel and concrete interior of the original (above) centres on a cast-iron Probat roaster – Sightglass is named after its viewing window. Incredibly, given this is California, there's no wi-fi. But once you savour the coffee, with a pistachio and blackberry croissant courtesy of Neighbor's Greg Mindel, you won't miss it one iota.
270 7th Street, T 861 1313,
www.sightglasscoffee.com

Bar Agricole

This smart bar/restaurant has long been considered one of the best cocktail spots in the US. Its culinary programme stalled after the departure of Brandon Jew (see p041), but it now has a reimagined menu with a northern California bent, sourcing ingredients from organic farms and using homegrown herbs. It is named after the cane-juice rum of the French Caribbean, and the drinks, built with craft spirits, are the main draw here; signatures include the Monkey's Gland (gin, grenadine, citrus and absinthe), and there's a selection of natural wines. Aidlin Darling Design broke up the long warehouse with a shell of reclaimed whisky-barrel oak, concrete banquettes and skylight installations of warped Pyrex cylinders. Brunch is served on Sundays.
355 11th Street, T 355 9400,
www.baragricole.co

Tawla

Restaurateur Azhar Hashem commissioned local architect Charles Hemminger and Minneapolis designers Cmnd+m to embody Tawla's The-Mission-meets-the-East-Med approach. Arabesque patterns subtly turn up throughout the 66-seat dining room, turquoise mosaic tiles and an installation of Turkish demitasses pay tribute to the region without resorting to kitsch, and the living wall, climbing up ornate latticework, introduces a Californian touch. Chef Joseph Magidow delves into the cuisines of Jordan, Lebanon, Palestine, Israel, Syria, Turkey, Greece and Iran, eschewing the ubiquitous hummus, falafel and tabbouleh. Instead, try beet *muhammara* and three *labnehs*, and standout mains like guinea hen *maraq temani*; the wine list is well travelled too. *206 Valencia Street, T 814 2704, www.tawlasf.com*

Rich Table

Although the moniker may lead you to think this restaurant pays homage to the Bay Area's celebrated fresh produce, it's actually named after husband-and-wife team Evan and Sarah Rich, who met at NYC's Bouley. Once they had familiarised themselves with Californian cuisine, he at foodie mecca Coi (T 393 9000), she at Michael Mina (T 397 9222), they opened this dinner-only temple to ingredient-driven dishes on the edge of Hayes Valley. Sardine chips and porcini doughnuts are specialities, and mains might well feature grilled Mount Lassen trout. The interiors by Said-Jon Eghbal are in keeping with the locavore ethos: wood is sourced from a Petaluma mill, and ceramics from Jered's Pottery, in Berkeley, and Heath (see p085). *199 Gough Street, T 355 9085, www.richtablesf.com*

Lazy Bear

Supper-club host David Barzelay turned his hobby into one of the most celebrated eateries in the country. The two-Michelin-starred Lazy Bear is a shared-dinner-party experience, for which you need to purchase tickets online (an entire month goes on sale at once, around the middle of the previous one). It has a mountain-lodge feel, thanks to charred wood walls, animal hides and a roaring fire. Mingle on the mezzanine for punch before taking a seat at the communal elm tables, which front the open kitchen. All-action staff whip up modern American dishes like scallop topped with sunflower petals, a shot of whipped eggs and maple syrup, and Wagyu ribeye with nettle. There are sittings at 6pm and 8.30pm, Tuesday to Saturday, for the 14-plus-course menu. *3416 19th Street, T 874 9921, www.lazybearsf.com*

Lord Stanley

What was once a stuffy Thai restaurant was reborn in 2015 as a 40-seat bistro with a British- and European-influenced menu and a mainly natural wine list. Thoughtful details bring warmth: the original timber pillars, a white concrete bar, custom birch tables, walnut-and-leather chairs, black ceramic light fixtures by local Mel Rice and a wool wall installation by Ashley Helvey. The eclectic aesthetics reflect the taste of husband-and-wife chefs Rupert and Carrie Blease, who opened their first venture after working in pedigreed kitchens like Per Se and Le Manoir aux Quat'Saisons. Inventive dishes have included ridgeback prawns, crumpet and seaweed butter; crispy duck leg and consommé, satsuma and rosemary; and rhubarb and elderflower custard tart. *2065 Polk Street, T 872 5512, www.lordstanleysf.com*

The Progress

Owners Stuart Brioza and Nicole Krasinski of hyper-hip State Bird Provisions (T 795 1272), which serves American small plates from roving carts, took their magic touch next door in 2014 to open a larger, slightly less casual (and easier to get into) eaterie with an Asian-accented Californian menu. The Progress has a buzzy, convivial feel, in part due to a 'family-style' dining concept, where each party is encouraged to share four main courses such as spiced beef and marrow pot-stickers (Chinese dumplings), butterbean and Spanish octopus ragout, and applewood-smoked squab. The venue is a conversion of the 1911 Progress theatre, spanning two levels underneath a glossy, curvy, double-height ceiling, and is decked out with wood cladding and potted plants. *1525 Fillmore Street, T 673 1294, www.theprogress-sf.com*

AL's Place

Since 2015, chef Aaron London's casual produce-driven eaterie has been one of the city's most sought-after reservations. AL's Place (the venue takes his initials) is quintessentially Californian for its focus on vegetable-centric and pescatarian cuisine. London applies the nose-to-tail dining concept to the garden, and mains have included sunchoke curry with black lime squid, citrus jewels and bergamot; and grits, goat's milk curds, chimichurri, figs, fennel and basil-bud mushrooms. Meats, like steak tartare with pickled kohlrabi and black mandarin, become sides – fitting in a state that prides itself on healthy eating and agriculture. Behind the bright-blue facade, plantlife, colourful chairs, paintings by Mission artist David Benzler and a tiny open kitchen animate the interior. A third of the seats are set aside for walk-ins.
1499 Valencia Street, T 416 6136,
www.alsplacesf.com

Boulibar

The Ferry Building foodie hub is anchored by Boulettes Larder, a breakfast, lunch and Sunday brunch institution known for its patio facing the Bay Bridge and finely crafted food and interior. In 2013, design firm Kallos Turin applied a similar ethos to the more casual Boulibar, which opens for lunch and dinner until 10pm Tuesday to Saturday. Oversized Tom Dixon pendant lights, a brass bead curtain, oak panelling and paintings by the local artist Deborah Oropallo, who is represented by Catharine Clark (see p070), set the tone. The kitchen sends out wood-fired pizzas, mezze and mains like swordfish. But topping the bill here are the craft cocktails, which come garnished with herb bitters or Japanese salted cherry blossoms. Closed Mondays. *1 Ferry Building, T 399 1155, The Embarcadero, www.bouletteslarder.com*

Benu

Corey Lee's three-Michelin-starred Benu is appropriately signposted by a street-facing kitchen, framed by the brick-arch windows of an ivy-clad 1922 building that was renovated by architect Richard Block. Through a Zen garden, the equally calm, understated interior features oak furniture embellished by custom-made ceramics from Kwangjuyo, hammered brass dishes and bespoke tableware, some of which is specifically tailored for certain courses, by local studio Blueoculus. In an exceptional tasting menu served Tuesday to Saturday evenings, Lee meshes his South Korean ancestry with classic French tradition in creations like jellyfish in beef bouillon, thousand-year-old quail egg, and faux shark-fin soup with Jinhua ham custard. *22 Hawthorne Street, T 685 4860, www.benusf.com*

Mourad

Working with local architect Olle Lundberg, chef Mourad Lahlou has reinterpreted the Marrakesh souks of his childhood by way of California inside the brick, concrete and steel shell of the art deco PacBell Building. Translucent backlit columns, mosaic tiles and perforated metalwork provide homage to his homeland. The cavernous space is a good bet for walk-ins, and buzzes with the tech business set (some wearing hoodies).

Highlights of the Michelin-starred menu include aubergine prepared three ways, sous-vide lamb shoulder, octopus with chickpeas, oranges, olives and merguez, and the signature basteeya, a flaky and nutty pastry filled with duck and lemon verbena. Or just stop by for a bourbon and cardamom cocktail at the well-stocked bar.
140 New Montgomery Street, T 660 2500, www.mouradsf.com

The Perennial

After setting up hipster favourites Mission Chinese Food (T 863 2800), where Danny Bowien's fiery Szechuan cuisine is served in an unreconstructed venue, and progressive farm-to-table fine-diner Commonwealth (T 355 1500), Anthony Myint and author wife Karen Leibowitz are pushing the eco envelope further. Their enterprise here champions carbon farming, aquaponics and the perennial grain Kernza (a wheat alternative), and the restaurant interior by Paul Discoe is a riot of reclaimed wood, along with recycled fabric, tiles, plaster and glass, and tableware of local clay. Chef Chris Kiyuna's fare includes pickled sardines, trout-belly 'bacon', and chicken with smoked parsnips and spinach, plated beautifully, if not a tad preciously.

59 9th Street, T 500 7788,
www.theperennialsf.com

Tartine Manufactory

Chad Robertson and Elisabeth Prueitt's cult bakery Tartine (T 487 2600) expanded into this corner site within the Heath Ceramics building in 2016. It's a hi-tech operation, with two grain mills and a massive German-built Heuft oven that places the artisanal process at the heart of this multi-tasking café, bar, ice-cream shop and restaurant. Architects Hemminger and LA-based firm Commune collaborated on the all-purpose space that resembles a Japanese carpentry shop, with high windows, industrial details and a neutral palette. Aside from the quite exemplary breads and patisserie, lunch encompasses pizzas, colourful salads and cobblers, and the dinner service features quality comfort food like rotisserie chicken, served on customised Heath tableware. *595 Alabama Street, T 757 0007, www.tartinemanufactory.com*

Trou Normand

Fine liquor aficionado Thad Vogler opened this follow-up to his lauded Bar Agricole (see p043) in 2014. As one would expect, libations here are top notch, with vintage cocktails (including the eponymous Trou Normand, concocted from rare armagnacs, cognacs and calvados), craft beers and an Old World-focused wine list. It's appetite-whetting stuff, and the kitchen is on hand with 40 types of house-cured charcuterie, plus chophouse-style grilled cuts. Located in the PacBell Building (see p055), a 1925 skyscraper by Timothy Pflueger, the dining room allows for casual encounters at the salvaged marble-top bar, beneath a giant nude by Ebecho Muslimova (above), which has been adopted as the logo, and more intimate affairs in tufted leather booths. *140 New Montgomery Street, T 975 0876, www.trounormandsf.com*

The Interval

This former metal workshop in Fort Mason, a 19th-century military base turned over for civilian use in 1972, was reinvented in 2014 as a café/bar run by The Long Now Foundation. Oakland studio Because We Can paid tribute to its past life, with touches of steampunk, original accoutrements like WWII-era surgery lights, and Atelier Dion's custom ceramics in British racing green, once the colour of the walls, now repainted white. The thick cocktail menu is a historical study (at times brainy, at other times pompous) into mixology, each page a genealogy of a certain drink, or themed, like a collection of concoctions associated with tiki bars. It gets rammed during the Off the Grid Friday-night food-truck meet, which takes place from April to October. *Landmark Building A, 2 Marina Boulevard, T 561 6582, www.theinterval.org*

Twenty Five Lusk
It can be hard to secure a dinner table at this celebrity haunt, but the lounge (right) is where you will want to see and be seen anyway; try to arrive before 7pm to beat the crowds. Designed by San Francisco architects CCS, it retains a strong sense of history; the building was originally a 1917 meatpacking house. Today, the restored exposed brickwork, wood beams and glass walls lend it a contemporary industrial edge, which is enhanced by suspended fire pits and long, low, curved banquettes. The cocktails here are first-class and get rave reviews, especially the Manhattan. If you do manage to secure a reservation in the dining room, expect New American cuisine with a European slant, courtesy of Matthew Dolan, who trained with Emeril Lagasse.
25 Lusk Street, T 495 5875,
www.twentyfivelusk.com

INSIDER'S GUIDE

CAROLINE ROONEY SERRANO, FASHION STYLIST

After relocating from New York in 2013, Caroline Rooney Serrano is now firmly settled in North Beach. 'San Francisco is a city with a big reputation and a small-town feel. As a young creative, there's a truly supportive community to plug into'. She likes to start a day at Mr Holmes Bakehouse (1042 Larkin Street, T 829 7700) in on-the-up Tenderloin. Nearby is the Jessica Silverman Gallery (see p030), which puts on 'the coolest openings', as well as Hero Shop (982 Post Street, T 829 3129): 'Former *Vogue* editor Emily Holt makes fashion downright fun, with great pieces across all price points.' Another top retail stop is Modern Appeal Clothing (1003 Minnesota Street, T 285 2805): 'The Ospital siblings are a local institution.'

To refuel, Rooney Serrano suggests Tartine Manufactory (see p057): 'The bread is to-die-for, but I go for cookies and ice cream.' And for dinner, she recommends Liholiho Yacht Club (871 Sutter Street, T 440 5446): 'The dishes are creative, and the open kitchen is so inviting.' She is also a big fan of Spruce (3640 Sacramento Street, T 931 5100), for a splurge, and Elephant Sushi (1916 Hyde Street, T 440 1905), although there's often a wait: 'I pop into Union Larder (1945 Hyde Street, T 323 4845) for a Grüner Veltliner.'

When she needs to get away, Rooney Serrano ups sticks to Scribe Winery (see p096) in Sonoma. 'Weekends there when I still lived in New York were a huge influence in my moving to San Francisco.' *For full addresses, see Resources.*

ART AND DESIGN
GALLERIES, STUDIOS AND PUBLIC SPACES

For a city of such global renown, San Francisco is small, less than a quarter the size of its rival LA, and has not fostered anywhere near as diverse an arts scene. But recently its tech wealth has catalysed a network of dealers and galleries, including blue-chip outliers like Gagosian (657 Howard Street, T 546 3990). Adding to a profusion of conventional display space, the lobbies of multinational firms here must be open to the public by law – the LinkedIn HQ (222 2nd Street), for instance, boasts three large Frank Stella paintings.

A thoroughly beefed-up SFMOMA (see p026) brought gravitas in 2016, while the sprawling Minnesota Street Project (see p068) injected further excitement. And in a pocket around Union Square, Jessica Silverman (see p030), Chandran (459 Geary Street, T 286 9533) and Haines (Suite 540, 49 Geary Street, T 397 8114), located in a building housing around 10 separate galleries, are proving that independents can thrive downtown, despite the rising rents.

The Bay Area's design industry isn't limited to sleek electronics. North California has a proud woodworking heritage, and Michael Taylor and John Dickinson became household names in the 1980s. Their legacy continues today with an emphasis on sustainable and reclaimed materials, seen in the output of artisans like Aleksandra Zee (www.aleksandrazee.com), who creates decorative geometric pieces. Workshop Residence (see p090) sells work by local makers. *For full addresses, see Resources.*

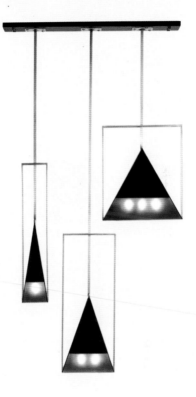

ShopFloor Design

Metal artist David Whippen opened his workshop in a low-slung factory in 2011, adding a by-appointment showroom in 2014 to exhibit limited-run pieces. The range is austere yet delicate, as seen in the powder-coated-steel 'Block Pendant' light (above), with its triangular shades framed by slender rectangles, and the 'Aurora' coffee table, a high-gloss black block. Sharing the space is microbrewery Harmonic (T 872 6817), whose bar opens Wednesday to Sunday. Many other San Francisco makers work with wood. Find midcentury-inspired walnut consoles at Jeremiah Collection (T 866 9554), while one-time Kyoto temple builder Paul Discoe fashions furniture from salvaged timber at Joinery Structures (T 510 451 6345). *1426 Minnesota Street, T 634 5306, www.shopfloordesign.com*

Guerrero Gallery

Hidden in a nursery south of Dogpatch,
Guerrero represents zeitgeisty US artists
John DeFazio, Shepard Fairey, Richard
Colman and Terry Powers. In the typically
irreverent show 'Copypasta' (pictured),
William Emmert, Isaac Avila Vazquez and
Adam Beris dissected painting through
reproduction and reorientation. It's open
Wednesdays to Saturdays, 12pm to 6pm.
1465 Custer Avenue, T 400 5168

Minnesota Street Project

A collective of studios and galleries has moved into this industrial complex (you can't miss it – the addresses are painted on the front in huge lettering). The soaring shed of 1275 Minnesota Street, with its girders, steel trusses and original wood-plank sawtooth ceiling, houses 11 full-time enterprises, from the established Anglim Gilbert to platforms for emerging talent like Bass & Reiner, and pieces are also strewn about the common areas (Anthony Discenza's *A Lapse Into The Romantic* in the atrium, above). Restaurant Alta serves executive chef Daniel Patterson's creative California cuisine. Nearby, little sister 1150 25th Street hosts Altman Siegel ('Rip or Rag' by Laeh Glenn, opposite; T 576 9300). Open Tuesdays to Saturdays, 11am to 6pm.
1275 Minnesota Street and 1150 25th Street, T 243 0825

Catharine Clark Gallery

Bringing a big-city edge to the SF scene, Catharine Clark is a leader in exhibiting experimental video art, and was the first gallery in town to feature a multimedia room. Showcasing contemporary work in six-week-long exhibits, the site displays a roster of established artists resident in the local area and beyond. These have included the sculptor Andy Diaz Hope, Deborah Oropallo, known for her paint-and-digital depictions of livestock, and Brooklyn-based Kambui Olujimi ('What Endures', above). In 2013, it relocated to an old factory in Potrero Flats, bolstering a growing art community there – while in the area, visit Hosfelt Gallery (T 495 5454), the Wattis Institute (see p036) and Yves Béhar's Fused Space (1401 16th Street).
*248 Utah Street, T 399 1439,
www.cclarkgallery.com*

Pier 24

Andy and Mary Pilara ignited a shared passion for photography with their first purchase, an image by Diane Arbus from Fraenkel Gallery (T 981 2661), in 2003. Seven years later, they launched Pier 24, which holds 5,000 photographs, one of the world's largest collections. The warehouse space is climate-controlled, and viewings are limited to 20 at a time; entry is free, but appointments must be booked online.

Themed shows – 'Secondhand' (above, works by Viktoria Binschtok and Joachim Schmid) explored found imagery – draw on a trove of canonical photographers (Lee Friedlander, Garry Winogrand) and contemporary practitioners (Todd Hido, Richard Learoyd). There are three two-hour visiting slots on Mondays to Fridays.
The Embarcadero, T 512 7424, www.pier24.org

ARCHITOUR

A GUIDE TO SAN FRANCISCO'S ICONIC BUILDINGS

The city's first golden age ended in rubble and smoke, when a 1906 earthquake and ensuing fire wiped out huge swathes of its Victorian stock. Those buildings that did survive (look around Alamo Square and Liberty Hill) continued to define the landscape for years.

Change was signalled by SOM's 1967 One Maritime Plaza (300 Clay Street) and the Transamerica Pyramid (see p013). However, the current construction frenzy is unprecedented. Inaugurated in 2005, Herzog & de Meuron's de Young Museum (see p031) created a halo effect, luring starchitects, and there was the cash to pay them, with Facebook hiring Frank Gehry for its 2015 Menlo Park HQ and Apple commissioning Foster + Partners for its 2017 Cupertino space station. Pelli Clarke Pelli designed the 2017 Transbay Transit Center interchange, a five-block-long 'floating' bubble with a roof garden, as well as the less inspiring Salesforce Tower (101 1st Street). This became the city's tallest structure in 2017, but simply confirmed that height doesn't seem to sit well here – the 197m Millennium Tower (301 Mission Street), from 2009, is similarly unremarkable, except for its sinking, earning it the inevitable Leaning Tower jokes.

The greatest success story is SFMOMA (see p026). But do seek out the smaller-scale gems, both new and old, from the stealth-like RMB (opposite) to the wonderful St Mary's (see p074), and Frank Lloyd Wright's 140 Maiden Lane, a proto-Guggenheim from 1948. *For full addresses, see Resources.*

UCSF Regeneration Medicine Building
Rafael Viñoly's cantilevered research lab snakes for 180m between the back of two 1960s towers and a road on the University of California's Parnassus campus. The slope reaches 45 degrees, making a build nigh-on untenable, yet engineers Nabih Youssef devised a steel-truss system that connects to deep concrete piles via base isolators, allowing a wobble of 26 inches in case of a quake. 'It is a site that essentially doesn't exist,' said Viñoly. 'At the time, California was one of the only states pursuing stem cell research. I loved this conspiracy theory that the building was hiding.' It opened in 2011, the only access being via a ninth-floor corridor through the Health Service tower and over a sky bridge. Circulation is aided by exterior flying ramps and stairs, which have fine views, as do four roof terraces.
35 Medical Center Way, stemcell.ucsf.edu

Cathedral of St Mary of the Assumption
One of the Catholic Church's boldest 20th-century statements, consecrated in 1971, St Mary's is the work of Italian-American modernist Pietro Belluschi, with engineer Pier Luigi Nervi and local architects Angus McSweeney, Paul A Ryan and John Michael Lee. Its travertine-faced concrete facade is inspired by a hyperbolic paraboloid, and soars 57m from four buttresses embedded into the bedrock – a square base rising to create a cross. The jaw-dropping interior emphasises the form and is given fluidity and dynamism by 1,680 triangular coffers in 128 sizes, and narrow banks of stained-glass windows designed by Gyorgy Kepes that ascend on four sides to converge at the apex. Sculptor Richard Lippold created the 45m-high baldachin using more than 4,000 aluminium rods. The impression it leaves is one of both drama and serenity.
111 Gough Street, T 567 2020,
www.stmarycathedralsf.org

BAMPFA, Berkeley

Diller Scofidio + Renfro's 2016 home for the Berkeley Art Museum and the Pacific Film Archive is a hybrid in every way – an interface between the university and the town, and a mashing together of a 1939 printing plant and a supple stainless-steel extension that slithers over the top to claim all the limelight. Yet the sawtooth roof of the original streamline modern building still allows light to penetrate the ground-floor galleries. At one end of the linear intervention is an LED screen and lawn for public viewings (left), although red tape means it's criminally under-used, and at the other, it tapers into a café that cantilevers over the entrance. Come for an art exhibition or to watch a film, and while you're here, check out its previous home, a brutalist Mario Ciampi structure nearby. It's a half-hour trip from Embarcadero.
2155 Center Street, T 510 642 0808, www.bampfa.berkeley.edu

Paramount Theatre, Oakland

Timothy Pflueger was the master of San Francisco art deco, and this 1931 theatre is as deliriously ornate as you'd imagine from its all-action multicoloured mosaic facade. In the awe-inspiring lobby (opposite), a green 'canopy' framed in gold, an amber 'fountain' and vermillion piers represent the sun breaking through a redwood forest. Intricate carvings, sumptuous signage and exuberant materials, including hand-adzed oak, Indonesian wood and Italian marble, abound throughout. The auditorium ceiling features motifs of Greek god Poseidon and Egyptian deity Isis, and in the ladies' make-up room (above), the walls are handpainted and even the vents are beautifully crafted. Catch a concert or a film, or take a tour on the first and third Saturdays of the month. *2025 Broadway, T 510 465 6400, www.paramounttheatre.com*

SHOPS

THE BEST RETAIL THERAPY AND WHAT TO BUY

San Francisco retailers have long championed handcrafted goods, exquisitely demonstrated at March (opposite), Joshu + Vela (see p083), design emporium The Future Perfect (3085 Sacramento Street, T 932 6508) and jewellery and ceramics gallery Esqueleto (482 49th Street, Oakland, T 510 629 6216). Also make a beeline for the interior stylings at Jay Jeffers – The Store (1035 Post Street, T 440 7300) and quirky stationery and gifts at Wishbone (601 Irving Street, T 242 5540). Major fashion brands like Marc Jacobs (No 125, T 362 6500) and Theory (No 120, T 399 1099) line pedestrianised Maiden Lane, and chic Fillmore Street, where you will find Freda Salvador (see p086) and Rag & Bone (No 2060, T 416 3978).

In this food utopia, edibles make great souvenirs. Buy gourmet treats at the Ferry Building (see p052); artisan chocolate from Fog City News (455 Market Street, T 543 7400); biodynamic wines at Terroir (1116 Folsom Street, T 558 9946); and for sustenance while you shop, sandwiches from Molinari Delicatessen (373 Columbus Avenue, T 421 2337). Rainbow Grocery Cooperative (1745 Folsom Street, T 863 0620) is the most right-on food store you'll ever visit.

Located in a former bowling alley, Amoeba Music (1855 Haight Street, T 831 1200), a vast indie shop, is a treasure trove of recorded product, while Western Relics (1400 Irving Street, T 759 5567), near Golden Gate Park (see p031), is more idiosyncratic.

For full addresses, see Resources.

March

Pots and pans assume art/design-object status at March, where Sam Hamilton sells skilfully crafted kitchenware made from the finest materials. Quality goods, such as a copper ladle by Detroit-based Smith Shop and Japanese oak trays by Azmaya, as well as covetable pantry items like own-brand Hawaii-harvested alder and hickory smoked salt, are beautiful products that epitomise the clean-lined aesthetic. The showroom is laid out as if it were a kitchen, with gleaming stainless-steel and copper fixtures, bespoke butcher-block tables from Matt Bear of Union Studio and an oxidised walnut bench by Sawkille (above). Hung on the walls are the marbled-ribeye paintings of Carrie Mae Smith alongside photos by New Yorker Paulette Tavormina. *3075 Sacramento Street, T 931 7433, www.marchsf.com*

Acacia

Former attorney Lily Chau left New York in 2011 and a year later set up this haven to stylish homewares. She's passionate about provenance and materials, and supports local independent artisans and designers. Displayed within the olive and cream walls, and on salvaged wood and pipe shelves, is an enticing edit of hand-thrown ceramics, decorative pieces, metalware, soft textiles and personal accessories. We were taken with the slick Bauhaus-inspired smoked-oak-veneer trivets and the coffee-making paraphernalia, including the stainless-steel and high-temperature-nylon 'Stagg Pour-Over Kettle' (above), $79, by Fellow Products, who are based in Dogpatch. Also available is Heliotrope's natural, organic, fragrance-free skincare. Closed Tuesdays. *415 Valencia Street, T 643 4847, www.acaciasf.com*

Joshu + Vela

After designing bags for Levi's and North Face, Noah Guy launched his own venture in 2010. Beautifully crafted leather and canvas rucksacks, duffels, totes, wallets and more are arranged attractively in the airy showroom, while in the back, his team works in plain view, cutting, stitching and riveting pieces in the atelier. Manufacturing on site, in batches as low as 20, facilitates experimentation with new products, while premium materials, including vegetable-tanned leather, military-spec hardware and extra-heavy canvas, will guarantee longevity. A favourite is the 'Boat Tote', with its hand-set copper details, bridle leather and 24oz cotton canvas, but we took home the merino-wool felt laptop sleeve trimmed with Horween leather. *3042 16th Street, T 872 5347, www.joshuvela.com*

Small Trade Company

Above the Heath Ceramics manufacturing/
retail complex, this is the workspace (part
showroom, part studio) of well-connected
creative Matt Dick. He designs apparel for
the hospitality industry, such as the staff
aprons for Tartine Manufactory (see p057)
downstairs, and Bar Agricole (see p043),
in addition to eminently wearable tunics
and kurtas with a Japanese accent – he
is fluent in the language and worked with
the legendary Tamotsu Yagi for eight years.
The atelier, which is shared with Heath
+ Stein bag-makers, is a window into his
animated mind: a mishmash of concrete
beams, patched-up wood floors, Japanese
geta clogs, mannequins and moodboard
walls. Dick also produces a range of denim,
leather and indigo-dyed cotton bags.
550 Florida Street D, T 570 1019,
www.smalltradecompany.com

Freda Salvador

In 2015, Sausalito-based designers Cristina Palomo-Nelson and Megan Papay relocated their flagship emporium to Fillmore Street. Their highly desirable yet durable range of women's shoes (perfect for San Francisco's topography) is handmade in Spain and borrows from classic men's styles, adding details including cut-outs, embossing and detachable fringes. 'We want to create the cool girl's everyday shoe – understated and effortless, bold and confident,' says Palomo-Nelson. Frequent collaborations produce capsule lines, such as the canvas kicks printed with geometric patterns by local artist Clare Rojas. The store is fitted out like a kooky apartment, with reclaimed wood, fluffy ottomans, threadbare rugs and curiosities like an upside-down 'foot' stool. *2416 Fillmore Street, T 872 9690, www.fredasalvador.com*

Local Mission Market

Sourcing produce solely from northern California (except for the spices, coffee, tea and chocolate), Local Mission Market's oak bins are filled with grains, chillies and fruit, and its butcher's counter alone is an education in sustainable farming. The list of suppliers reads like a *Who's Who* of the region's organic champions – fish reeled in year-round by Captain Morgan from Half Moon Bay, or sun-dried pluots courtesy of

Nick and Marissa of Cipponeri Family Farms in Turlock. On week nights, it also serves hot dishes like braised oxtail and sweet-and-spicy squash. Be sure to try the Tilted Shed Smoked cider, made from a blend of six varieties of Sonoma County heirloom and wood-smoked apples, at sister store Local Cellar (T 795 4022) round the corner.
2670 Harrison Street, T 795 3355, www.localmissionmarket.com

Song Tea & Ceramics

Peter Luong, whose parents ran a veteran Chinatown apothecary, takes a sommelier-like approach to the brew. Each spring, he introduces a new selection of teas, chosen for their 'structure, texture, character and complexity', sourced from independent producers in China and Taiwan, and runs regular tasting sessions on a first-come-first-served basis ($10). The store, on a residential street in Lower Pacific Heights, amalgamates midcentury modern style and a Japanese aesthetic, with furniture by local carpenter Blair Haffly. Porcelain canisters are filled with loose leaves, and exquisite ceramics are presented neatly on wooden blocks – the hand-formed unglazed 'Zisha' clay teapots are made in Jiangsu. Closed Mondays ('drinking tea'). *2120 Sutter Street, T 885 2118, www.songtea.com*

Workshop Residence

This pioneering company collaborates with emerging and renowned global designers, and partners with local manufacturers to produce functional goods. Craftsman Paul Discoe (see p065) transformed a former stable, framing the entrance with salvaged black acacia wood and hanging 12m-long pine shelves from the ceiling. The founder, Ann Hatch, stained the raw floors in bright patterns, while a modular concrete 'I-Block'

wall was designed by Jim Isermann, whose screen-printed utility blankets are on sale. Also on offer here are items like hand-built tubs by Michael Parker, necklaces in slip-cast ceramic by fashion designer Aurore Thibout, black basalt 'Crockery' by Max Lamb, and hand-sewn *yukata* (a light cotton kimono) by Sendai-based Tsuyo Onodera. *833 22nd Street, T 285 2050, www.workshopresidence.com*

Root Science

Hailing from a family with sensitive skin, Icelander Gigja Hlín Wesneski resolved to find a solution, inspired by her homeland's affinity to nature. Based in north California, her botanical skincare line is packed with vitamin-rich oils from organic plants and herbs that are cold-pressed to preserve their integrity and nutrients. The 'Youth' moisturiser and serum (above), $120 for 30ml, is a blend of passionfruit and jojoba seed oils, and the 'Polish' facial exfoliant contains turmeric root, rice flour and detoxifying clays. As no preservatives or artificial fragrances are used, the range is produced in micro-batches, and the dark violet glass containers block out sunlight to maintain potency. Packaging features an abstracted mountain landscape. The company ships to the UK, France and Italy. *www.shoprootscience.com*

William Stout Architectural Books
There is no telling how this bookshop, dedicated to architecture, art and design, stays open in the age of Amazon, but it doesn't seem to be going anywhere any time soon. Just one block away from the Transamerica Pyramid (see p013), it was founded by architect William Stout more than three decades ago. On his return from Europe, books unavailable in San Francisco in hand, he found that friends would ask him to acquire copies for them too. So he opened this store, which today is stuffed with more than 20,000 tomes that run the gamut of creative subjects, from graphic design and typography to landscaping and the decorative arts. The knowledgeable staff will help you find a rare edition or simply leave you to browse. *804 Montgomery Street, T 391 6757, www.stoutbooks.com*

Self Edge

Specialising in Japanese selvedge denim (Iron Heart, The Flat Head, 3sixteen), Self Edge is an interesting space to visit even if you are not in the market for dropping several hundred dollars on a pair of jeans. It stocks an impressive variety of brands rarely seen outside Japan, although there are more options for men than women. Complimentary hemming is available on all purchases, achieved using a vintage chain-stitching machine. The denim range is the focal point, but there's also a good selection of men's shirts and accessories. Founded in 2006 by Bay Area husband-and-wife team Kiya and Demitra Babzani, Self Edge has proved a real hit, and has expanded across the States, with outlets in New York, Los Angeles and Portland. *714 Valencia Street, T 558 0658, www.selfedge.com*

Dandelion Chocolate

Founded by Silicon Valley whizzkids Todd Masonis and Cameron Ring, Dandelion takes pride in the fact that its product is made using only two ingredients – cocoa beans and organic cane sugar – and it roasts, cracks, sorts, winnows, grinds, conches and tempers small batches on-site. The result is intensely rich bars that honour the nuances of their terroir, which could be Ambanja in Madagascar (fruity), the Maya Mountains in Belize (caramel-like) or Alta Verapaz in Guatemala (nutty). Equally tasty are the morsel-sized pastries, such as the huckleberry macaron, crafted by pastry chef Lisa Vega, in the café. The rapidly expanding brand is headquartered in a former auto repair shop, and has high ceilings, wood rafters and exposed brick. *740 Valencia Street, T 349 0942, www.dandelionchocolate.com*

No 3

Jenny Chung's retail outlets have injected some sartorial sass into her native city. Whereas Chung's original store, Acrimony (T 861 1025), which launched in 2008, is dedicated to mens- and womenswear and accessories by emerging and hard-to-find labels, No 3 is focused wholly on jewellery, displaying each designer's collection in a glass terrarium created by local craftsman Conor Sweitzer. Expect an assemblage of sculptural pieces, such as the gold-plated-brass and rubber double-helix bracelet by Faux/Real, and more delicate items, like an interlocking puzzle ring by NYC brand Bliss Lau, as well as statement costume jewellery. Those considering popping the question should check out the unorthodox engagement rings with singular settings. *1987 Hyde Street/Union Street, T 525 4683, www.shopno3.com*

ESCAPES

WHERE TO GO IF YOU WANT TO LEAVE TOWN

The scenery around San Francisco is some of the most arresting in America. Admire it by renting a bike and cycling north over the Golden Gate Bridge (see p010) to the vantage point on the far side overlooking the city, or beyond to the Marin Headlands and Rodeo Beach, where you can visit the Headlands Center for the Arts (944 Simmonds Road, Sausalito, T 331 2787). For a sublime connection with nature, make for Muir Woods in Mill Valley, some 15km north of the bridge. Its majestic redwoods are some of the tallest trees on the planet. Point Reyes National Seashore, 50km north-west of the city, is stunning, its cliffs towering above beautiful stretches of sand. Hamlets here, like Bolinas, are the epitome of moneyed hippiedom. Locals remove road signs in the hope that visitors won't find them.

One of the world's great drives is south down the Pacific Coast Highway to Carmel and Big Sur. Perched 365m above the ocean, Post Ranch Inn (47900 Highway 1, T 800 527 2200) is on the bucket list of most San Franciscans. North of town, on the other hand, is wine country. Choosing between Napa (see p100) and Sonoma (see p101) is tough, but someone's got to do it; perhaps plump for the latter for its variety of landscapes and hyper-local cuisine. Head for Scribe Winery (2100 Denmark Street, T 707 939 1858), which is known for its chardonnay and hip vibe, and the French-accented bistro The Girl & The Fig (110 West Spain Street, T 707 938 3634). *For full addresses, see Resources.*

Windhover, Stanford

This students' sanctuary was inserted into the Stanford University campus in 2014. It revolves around the contemplative power of the five 'Windhover' paintings by Nathan Oliveira. These massive canvases created from the 1970s are named after Gerard Manley Hopkins' 1877 poem and inspired by kestrels that swoop over the foothills. Aidlin Darling Design's unobtrusive pavilion exists solely as a vehicle for the art, with its clean lines, natural light, reflecting pond, earthen walls, weathered steel, pebbled patios, stone sculptures and wood benches. Landscaped by Andrea Cochran, the site incorporates an oak glade, ginkgo trees, a bamboo grove, and a labyrinth meditation path. Tours are held on Saturdays at 11am. It's a 40-minute drive south to Stanford. *370 Santa Teresa Street, T 650 723 1762, windhover.stanford.edu*

Marin County Civic Center, San Rafael

Frank Lloyd Wright's last design, the Marin County Civic Center, is 32km north of San Francisco. Completed after the architect's death by his protégé Aaron Green, and situated on an old dairy farm, the building bears all of Wright's hallmarks. The arches, dome and cut-outs echo the topography of the site, and the sandy colour of the walls resembles the shade of the earth. Inside, corridors with rounded corners create the illusion of a continuous circular space. The most distinctive feature, a 52.4m gold-anodised spire, separates the hall of justice and administration wings. Time your visit in order to coincide with Marin's oldest farmers' market, held on Thursday and Sunday mornings in the car park, but due to receive a permanent $20m plot.
10 Avenue of the Flags, T 473 6400, www.marincounty.org

Turnbull, Oakville

Oakville in the Napa Valley, 100km north of San Francisco, has only about 70 residents but two dozen wineries. At the family-run Turnbull estate, architect William Turnbull Jr's redwood timber structures provide a stripped, contemporary take on shingle-and-wood-siding barns. Inside, warm plaids and browns create a cosy ambience in the tasting room, where photography by Herb Ritts, Dorothea Lange and Edward Weston lines the walls. Drop by between 9am and 5pm to sample the small-batch cabernet sauvignon and sauvignon blanc. Just south of here, otherwise modest Yountville is a world-renowned gourmet destination, due to Michelin-starred The French Laundry (T 707 944 2380) and Bouchon Bistro (T 707 944 8037), both by Thomas Keller. *8210 St Helena Highway, T 707 963 5839, www.turnbullwines.com*

SingleThread, Healdsburg

Even in Sonoma County, where farm-to-table is a given, this restaurant/inn stands out for its intimate link to the soil. Katina Connaughton cultivates speciality produce including ginger, aubergine, lily bulbs, figs and olives (the rest comes from the expert Sonoma growers), and husband Kyle, a Fat Duck and Toya Japon alumnus, marinates, sous-vides and experiments in the kitchen. Their north California take on the *kaiseki* experience begins with appetisers in the rooftop herb garden, followed by 11 courses in the dining room, where woven screens represent the DNA sequence of 12 seasonal vegetables, while the glazed-tile walls in the lounge were made using local clay. The ceramics are from Nagatani-en in Iga, Japan. Healdsburg is 110km north of San Francisco. *131 North Street, T 707 723 4646, www.singlethreadfarms.com*

THE FAIREST PICTURE
THE WHOLE EARTH AFFORDS
—MARK TWAIN

Coachman Hotel, Lake Tahoe

This ageing motel, built for the 1960 Winter Olympics, was treated to a modish reboot in 2016, courtesy of Brooklyn's Studio Tack, who installed rustic plywood carpentry, and a convivial lobby bar (opposite) with ski-lodge styling and large bifold windows that open out onto the outdoor swimming pool, fire pits and hot tubs. The 42 rooms (above) have handcrafted platform beds with Frette linens and handy rubber wet areas for snowgear, boots and swimsuits. The region traditionally attracts gamblers, who head over the state line to Nevada to bet, but offers a host of outdoor activities, from pristine pistes to horse-riding, hiking, ballooning and wine-tasting on a vintage cabin cruiser. South Lake Tahoe is a four-hour drive north-east of San Francisco.
4100 Pine Boulevard, T 530 545 6460, www.coachmantahoe.com

NOTES

SKETCHES AND MEMOS

RESOURCES

CITY GUIDE DIRECTORY

A

ABV 024
3174 16th Street
T 400 4748
www.abvsf.com

Acacia 082
415 Valencia Street
T 643 4847
www.acaciasf.com

Acrimony 095
333 Hayes Street
T 861 1025
www.shopacrimony.com

AL's Place 050
1499 Valencia Street
T 416 6136
www.alsplacesf.com

Altman Siegel 068
1150 25th Street
T 576 9300
www.altmansiegel.com

Americano 020
Hotel Vitale
8 Mission Street
T 278 3777
www.hotelvitale.com

Amoeba Music 080
1855 Haight Street
T 831 1200
www.amoeba.com

Anchor Brewing Company 036
1705 Mariposa Street
T 863 8350
www.anchorbrewing.com

Audio 040
316 11th Street
T 481 0556
www.audiosf.com

B

BAMPFA 076
2155 Center Street
Berkeley
T 510 642 0808
www.bampfa.berkley.edu
Closed Mondays and Tuesdays

Bar Agricole 043
355 11th Street
T 355 9400
www.baragricole.com

Benjamin Cooper 022
Hotel G
398 Geary Street
www.benjamincoopersf.com

Benu 053
22 Hawthorne Street
T 685 4860
www.benusf.com

Bergerac 040
316 11th Street
T 255 9440
www.bergeracsf.com

Bouchon Bistro 100
6534 Washington Street
Yountville
T 707 944 8037
www.thomaskeller.com/
bouchonyountville

Boulibar 052
1 Ferry Building
The Embarcadero
T 399 1155
www.bouletteslarder.com

C

California Academy of Sciences 032
55 Music Concourse Drive
T 379 8000
www.calacademy.org

HOTELS

ADDRESSES AND ROOM RATES

The Battery 021
Room rates:
double, from $500;
Lounge Suite, from $900;
Penthouse, from $10,000
717 Battery Street
T 230 8000
www.thebatterysf.com/hotel

The Buchanan 018
Room rates:
double, from $200;
King Balcony, from $225
1800 Sutter Street
T 921 4000
www.thebuchananhotel.com

Clift 016
Room rates:
double, from $220
495 Geary Street
T 775 4700
www.morganshotelgroup.com

Coachman Hotel 102
Room rates:
double, from $150
4100 Pine Boulevard
Lake Tahoe
T 530 545 6460
www.coachmantahoe.com

Hotel G 022
Room rates:
double, from $230;
Greatest King Suite, from $260
386 Geary Street
T 738 0589
www.hotelgsanfrancisco.com

Inn at the Presidio 016
Room rates:
double, from $300
42 Moraga Avenue
T 800 7356
www.innatthepresidio.com

InterContinental 016
Room rates:
double, from $260
888 Howard Street
T 616 6500
www.intercontinentalsanfrancisco.com

Mystic Hotel 016
Room rates:
double, from $300
417 Stockton Street
T 400 0500
www.mystichotel.com

Phoenix 016
Room rates:
double, from $170
601 Eddy Street
T 776 1380
www.jdvhotels.com

Post Ranch Inn 096
Room rates:
double, from $875
47900 Highway 1
Big Sur
T 800 527 2200
www.postranchinn.com

The Ritz-Carlton 016
Room rates:
double, from $400
600 Stockton Street
T 296 7465
www.ritzcarlton.com

St Regis
Room rates:
double, from $680
125 3rd Street
T 284 4000
www.stregissanfrancisco.com

Tilden Hotel
Room rates:
double, from $200
345 Taylor Street
T 673 2332
www.tildenhotel.com

Hotel Vitale
Room rates:
double, from $275;
Terrace Suite, from $525;
Deluxe Panoramic Circular Suite,
from $700
8 Mission Street
T 278 3700
www.hotelvitale.com

Zeppelin
Room rates:
double, from $300;
Deluxe Suite, from $600
545 Post Street
T 563 0303
www.viceroyhotelsandresorts.com

Zetta
Room rates:
double, from $230
55 5th Street
T 543 8555
www.hotelzetta.com

WALLPAPER* CITY GUIDES

Executive Editor
Jeremy Case

Author
Chaney Kwak

Deputy Editor
Belle Place

Photography Editor
Rebecca Moldenhauer

Junior Art Editor
Jade R Arroyo

Editorial Assistant
Charlie Monaghan

Contributor
Cheryl Locke

Intern
Nicole Albers

Production Controller
Nick Seston

**Marketing & Bespoke
Projects Manager**
Nabil Butt

Wallpaper*® is a
registered trademark
of Time Inc (UK)

First published 2007
Sixth edition 2017

© Phaidon Press Limited

All prices and venue
information are correct
at time of going to press,
but are subject to change.

Original Design
Loran Stosskopf
Map Illustrator
Russell Bell

**Wallpaper*
Editor-in-Chief**
Tony Chambers

Contacts
wcg@phaidon.com
@wallpaperguides

More City Guides
www.phaidon.com/travel

Phaidon Press Limited
Regent's Wharf
All Saints Street
London N1 9PA

Phaidon Press Inc
65 Bleecker Street
New York, NY 10012

Phaidon® is a registered
trademark of Phaidon
Press Limited

www.phaidon.com

A CIP Catalogue record for
this book is available from
the British Library.

Printed in China

ISBN 978 0 7148 7482 1

PHOTOGRAPHERS

Henrik Kam
San Francisco city view, inside front cover
Golden Gate Bridge, pp010-011
Coit Tower, p012
Federal Building, pp014-015
Zeppelin, p017
The Buchanan, p018, p019
Hotel G, pp022-023
Mazarine Coffee, p025
SFMOMA, p026
Contemporary Jewish Museum, p027
Onsen, p028
California Academy of Sciences, pp032-033
The David Ireland House, p034, p035
San Francisco Center for the Book, p036
Street art, p037
Saison, pp038-039
Mister Jiu's, p041
Sightglass, p042
Bar Agricole, p043
Tawla, p044
Rich Table, p045
Lazy Bear, pp046-047
Lord Stanley, p048

The Progress, p049
AL's Place, pp050-051
Benu, p053
Mourad, p054, p055
The Perennial, p056
Tartine Manufactory, p057
Trou Normand, p058
The Interval, p059
Twenty Five Lusk, pp060-061
Caroline Rooney Serrano, p063
Minnesota Street Project, p068, p069
Cathedral of St Mary of the Assumption, p074
BAMPFA, pp076-077
Paramount Theatre, p078, p079
March, p081
Small Trade Company, pp084-085
Freda Salvador, p086
Local Mission Market, p087
Song Tea & Ceramics, pp088-089
Workshop Residence, p090
William Stout Architectural Books, p092
Self Edge, p093
Dandelion Chocolate, p094
No 3, p095

Joe Fletcher
Cathedral of St Mary of the Assumption, p075

Matthew Millman
Windhover, p097

Mariko Reed
Boulibar, p052

James Reid
Transamerica Pyramid, p013

Raquel Venancio
Onsen, p029

Arcaid Images/Alamy
Marin County Civic Center, p099

ArchitecTour/Alamy
Marin County Civic Center, p098

Fine Arts Museums of San Francisco
de Young Museum, p031

SAN FRANCISCO
A COLOUR-CODED GUIDE TO THE HOT 'HOODS

NORTH BEACH/CHINATOWN
Encompassing beatnik bookshops, upscale eateries and the oldest Chinatown in the US

NOB HILL
This affluent neighbourhood of storied mansions has some of the city's best panoramas

DOGPATCH
Due to a clutch of exciting galleries, this scrappy enclave is becoming a cultural player

SOMA
Leading museums and swanky condos for the technorati cluster in the centre of town

FINANCIAL DISTRICT
Discreetly chic establishments cater for all the office workers in the skyscrapers above

THE TENDERLOIN/UNION SQUARE
Part gritty, part swanky, these few blocks summarise San Francisco's differing faces

THE MISSION
Of-the-now bars, fine restaurants and indie boutiques have redefined the Latin quarter

HAYES VALLEY
Dotted with interesting venues, Hayes Street and its environs are a shopaholic's dream

For a full description of each neighbourhood, see the Introduction.
Featured venues are colour-coded, according to the district in which they are located.